THE LONELY-WILDS

Wick Poetry Chapbook Series Four
Maggie Anderson, Editor

How to Paint the Savior Dead
Jason Gray

The Space Between Stars
Matt McBride

Spotlit Girl
Kevin Oberlin

Tornado
Ted Lardner

Song of the Rest of Us
Mindi Kirchner

Salt
Liz Tilton

The List of Dangers
Maggie Smith

So, how was the war?
Hugh Martin

Tethering World
Jody Rambo

The Lonely-wilds
Elizabeth Breese

THE LONELY-WILDS

Poems by Elizabeth Breese

The Kent State University Press
Kent, Ohio

© 2011 by Elizabeth Breese
Library of Congress Catalog Card Number 2010036310
ISBN 978-1-60635-070-6
Manufactured in the United States of America

The Wick Poetry Series is sponsored in part by the Wick Poetry Center at Kent State University.

Library of Congress Cataloging-in-Publication Data
Breese, Elizabeth.
The lonely-wilds : poems / by Elizabeth Breese.
p.   cm. — (Wick poetry chapbook series four)
ISBN 978-1-60635-070-6 (pbk. : alk. paper) ∞
I. Title.
PS3602.R4435166 2011
811'.6—dc22

2010036310

British Library Cataloging-in-Publication data are available.

15 14 13 12 11   5 4 3 2 1

For my grandmothers

CONTENTS

ACKNOWLEDGMENTS

My thanks to the editors of the following journals where some of these poems first appeared:

Barrow Street: "Subsidy"
FIELD: "Grenora, N.D.," "Supernature," "Calamity the way I think it," and
        "Self-portrait at Glendalough"
Sou'wester: "Amen"

I am grateful for the Vorman Scholarship Fund from the Department of English at The Ohio State University, which made the research for several of these poems possible.

For their help and wisdom, I would like to thank Kathy Fagan, Andrew Hudgins, Angie Estes, and Henri Cole. Thank you to my dear friends at The Ohio State University for their tremendous support and kindness. Claire and Annie, you've been true blue.

To my parents, thank you for encouraging me always.

ARS POETICA

The best & worst things happen here,
but everyone loves the idea of honey. So here
is my little bee hand in pocket editions, the rough-
cut paper combs, dancing for the things it loves.
The worst things are voices, wrong
somehow & sour. If it is not elderly enough to totally
crack its hips in my closed hand, I think of the long
limping walk toward disaster.
The voice of the sensual, if it does not crack
someone's hips, will be put to bed
without a kiss. It must fight the urge to turn
over & ask what it did wrong until it falls asleep.
The worst things are all true; I have been the girl
whose bones are the hull of a ship called
lost at sea many times. The worst things are false
or thankless like a dachshund. I can still see
the hands of German breeders pulling the spines
long & the badgers quaking underground.
If I ever invent a metaphor
that frightens a badger, I'll put a choker on it.
There are good things to let loose
in the backyard, but the best things are alimental,
without water or added sweeteners. Come raw,
crystallized, or strained. Come from a wide-mouth
jar. They drip slow from my mouth & hands,
pool like cardinals & mudras
on the page. I hear someone I love arrive
slowly. I hear her dialect of sagesse. A panacea,
it comes still infused with pollen & propolis;
the best things come clung to.
They may or may not cure hay fever,
but when they come along, I expose my soft palate
in the garden. I part my lashes among the ragweed,
last name ambrosia.

GRENORA, N.D.

The man I was had neighbors;
the couple from Montana croaked.

Now in those houses the snow & cats drift.
   The horses & fields grow
   lonely-wild together.

So many who came with the trains
the Bowl laid flat—that was dark times,
with night for days.

Our baby girl, only girl, was stillborn
& the three boys lived & left. When I die,
someone young in town will be oldest.
   It is unfair to be so young
   & made so old.

People can grow lonely-wild, too,
but not the man I am. I've got a radio.

CALAMITY THE WAY I THINK IT

The radio is a brown jug
puffing world news over my shoulder.

I will hear it before I feel it; sooner
or later, a tornado will come

for everyone who knows
my love language is non sequiturs.

Everyone to the tub, where I shower
with my houseplants,

clog the drain & drown the burro's tail.
Everyone in the ditch,

cover your heads. I would be a dolphin
before even a benign shark.

You in the crawlspace, I am listening.
I am in bed developing safety

rituals with rose & cedar candles.
I hand crank my radio beyond

its lethargic batteries. Oh, Most National
Weather Service, be with them—

the lover who knows I hate cooking
for myself, who knows I get marooned

at the counter by a bag of lentils,
who knows, unattended, I only eat

Cheerios in pink yogurt.
The cousin with a therapy cat.

The friend with snowflake tattoos
on her neck. The parents.

Everyone in the basement with flash-
lights & important papers, everyone

lodged beneath the overpass
I am all ears & yours through the sirens

but I am certain it will end, sooner
or later, with me saying nothing to no one.

NORTHERN PASTORAL

I put distinctive pinecones on the mantle.
I fight the resin gloves from my hands
in the kitchen. If we argue, bring me
wild onions every day for all the sorries.
Bring me lupines, bring kindling in birch bark
garters. Bring the water spider outside, please.
Answer where the birds go in a tornado when
I worry about it. We live the daytime of osprey
& eagle, the gray hours of deer, the all night of
unseen travelers. The dead mouse is ripe inside
the electric blankets whose bright potential
keeps me restless anyway. I will canoe us
perpendicular through the wake, swear & canoe us
away from the noise. We are the motorless
purists. For joining me in the woods, where
I am not even from, I think you are radiant.
The spirit of the place is inside me forever—
the zebra mussel's benevolent cousin.
Radiance, where does your best heart reside?
Is there a faint glow you see coming over
the curve of the equator? Does it come from a
beacon pasture, city, or stadium in your snippet
of a country? Are your pockets empty for bus passes
or desert salt crystals from the Atacama?
Radiance, let me accompany you to some place
Spanish for *this is what I was talking about.*

CHILE

The city air is porridge
in the earth bowl. In summer,
     everyone goes to breathe
     in the ocean.
We go, too.

The hotelier makes me
a practical dirty joke:
     un watero con uñas.
Si, complimentary.
     I come with the room.

I find copper & lapis lazuli
     between my toes & in my ears
     every night before bed.
You crash onto the beach, into bed,
into me, break into Spanish.

You are a native son even with me
burning in the sun at your side.
You bring me home
to a riddle on the coast:
     I am not an island, though
     I is land. Still, I am to the gills
     with seashells. Still, I hold a boat.
     I am in poems. Poems are in me.
     I am only black on the map.
     What am I?

You are Isla Negra,
     a roomy museum.
No, you are home. You are
la cocina, my living room,
the garden full of poppies.

begins with questions. Did you know
there was open soil to my brain?
Did you see my hair all dusted up?
Because someone has thrown into it rusty
scraps & now I'm alkaline, shriveled blue
from the earth up. My mophead falls
against my chest, my knees fall into my
arms. I am weird & incapable of holding
myself up for the morning, for you.
Make me a trowel & an arc of blisters
against the oxidized hubcap & the sub-
terranean cairn of bolts. Make me
a diligent digger. I will lay it all,
now unreactive, on the lawn.
May we, who uncovered the Hoard
of Unannounced Terror, sell it
to the National Museum to see it under
glass & surveillance. Fingering the dirt
away from my nape, may I turn pink—
enamored with levity.

SUPERNATURE

I met my grandmother again. She was preening
in the neighbors' yard.

She is all the vermillion males in the world,
designed to be noticed today in the pagoda dogwood.

She sings affirmations to the tune of *always*
& *of course, what else could ever be?*

My heart is run ragged. She charges
the crow from its perch; nature is nurture.

Our roots send up wings, antlers, & fins
that nature us through the rest.

AMEN

Little bird who fell
from its nest at the height of gutters

& spring, you are
the pink kamikaze on my bottom stair.

You are the anty baby.

Sparrow, I think,
you would have been average. Now,

I am thinking of songs

in significant Latin, which is all wrong
except we are in the alley

behind St. Francis of Assisi Church.
What language was he speaking

to the birds in the trees?
No, not pidgin, little bird.

That was all wrong.
I could never say a prayer, though.

I will put you in the grass. I will put

you in a poem, where you will be happy

to know your dad kept a tiny vigil,
& your mom could not bear

to mention your name.

SUBSIDY

I live hand to mouth
from my father's hand.
He is generous, I am
Helena Handbasket.
We write in serifs,
charcoal, & ventriloquy:
the dog says hello.
My father wants to live
in a silo & draw rabbits
smoking cigarettes
on the walls & eat herring
raw. There, we'd speak
with fear of the practical life
he might have lived.

We write of repairs.
Dad, your crushed eye
socket, the delirium
tremens, my, my, my
overdraft, my hopes
are flimsy & flaking
like mica that you'll survive
your regrets. Daughter,
my regrets look like me
at the hands of my father's
basement buzz cut.
Look, I wish I was living
hopefully, like you,
but with acrylic.

I am the child of
his reckless dreams.
I grow my hair long.
I wax impractical &
catalogue the words
I cannot stand—*dregs,*
scrim, scum—
for a good time.
I live letter to letter
when he ghost-prospects;
hello, says the dog,
save a little of this.

FONTANEL

Penelope Pureheart was born under a star
that has her by the tear ducts & the soft parts
even crustaceans keep covered. Her smoke-thin
skin lets meteors the size of absconded buttons,
dying rabbits, & minor & major chords break
through in tearful, bright shows we cannot predict
or quell. Her sighs are splinters in our fingertips;
we hurt, we are touched. We wish for relief, for how
will she live day to day knowing this star is dying?
Astronomy isn't for the faint of heart, we hint,
but our daughter has dark eyes, not foreseeing.
It is my day to watch the cosmos for any peaked or
misshapen crocus in the ditch so it may be plucked
& composted before Penelope is undone.

BEVERLY & DORIS, 1990

We should have these ditch flowers
in our heads like

the geriatric dementia rolling around.

I never remember blue chicory
in the moment. You are always pointing at it.

Are you thinking you might be next? I am.

I am in your Florida home about this time every year.

The crocus was just poking through when
I left. You hem my pants, so when I go back

they won't slush up. Thank you.

Do you recognize the old me? Are these shades of
our old mother sprouting?

I am your brown-eyed Susan, sister.

You are my oldest friend, but don't ask me
to pick up the violin.

I won't go revisiting youth with a thorn
in my side or a bow in my hand & streaky tears.

What is your middle name? Whoever goes down this

crumbling path first
gets to eat as many funSize Snickers as they want.

Let's go for a walk & not get lost. On this one,
I will keep my bearings

straight from
the waxy leaves, the skittering lizards everywhere,

the promise of afternoon thunderheads.

You are my best friend, but will we know
who to miss? Will you know me in starts-&-stops?

Will we remember if the other has passed? Or,
will we keep shaking our heads?

MURRAY RIVER,

My wife is at the window, watching me watch everything dusted & blowing away. She returns—afraid of what she'll find—every few hours. I cannot find her there again.

We are at Swan Hill. Remember the stone-fruit trees? The branches never bend low enough to make money. We were with you before the armada of weirs & locks, before the drought. We were with you before they ran you out, into the ocean. Once, we were prodigal. Now, you are a salty vein.

All of this is just to say I am as surprised as you.

She will find me in the orchard; if I become afraid in the moment, let me fall face-first. I am too young to be dead—many will say so—but the world has changed & rivers disappear. This is no place to be without hope.

If this is the one you hear, there's nothing left. I cracked the trunks of many trees to give the strongest a chance, even they are charred by the sun. I will remember you with silver perch & bony bream. I will remember you without salt. You in the orchard, in the roots of the trees, in the fruit in our hands. Remember me with my hands full.

—Friend, because I feel you gone every day.

HER PORTRAIT BY ALAN LOMAX

This calloused workday song evolved
over days & months to include harrowing details:
    a love lost
    not in the ocean
    nor to a bullet.

His name was likely not Brandon,
but for posterity they rhymed the man & his verb.

People are willing archivers.
    We whistle while at work
    & never wonder what.

Brandon, in this case, decided he'd had enough.
In other melodies, he contracts wanderlust,
a wandering eye, a hole in his wallet.

A folk song is an address; you've landed here.
    We sing through our noses,
    & lock our doors at night.
    Our girls are pale-skinned,
    but what rhymes with *high and dry?*

CENOTAPH

In winter, it was the sweat-slam of fishing
beneath good yarn. In summer, he was doomed
to hurry after good weather. Either a marvel or morose,
his guide is still the sky, but now he's driving day-trippers
with babies in a jaunting car after ruins. This is the Iron Age
fort. This is a beehive hut. No mortar in the walls.
His mouth is a spade uncovering details; in the winter,
it was the sweat-slam. Today his winch & nets haul nothing,
but there are sweaters, scarves, & small freshly arranged
mittens near the ferry. He takes the family past
cenotaphs of old island families. *Hernon. Conneely.*
He takes the family photo in front of *Gill*. Beneath the high
cross, two boys play accordion & banjo. Their sister keeps
the rhythm in Kerry style. This is a reel. This is the Kildare
Fancy. His eyes are on the cloudy dogma of a late-summer
sky. There are two ferries yet to depart Ros a' Mhíl,
but a cold rain keeps visits hurried & sloppy behind a horse.
What is this cheerful flower, & this? He identifies
orange Montbretia & Russian vine, a climber.

INIS ÓIRR

From this slip of land near the sun,
I lost my solace & my spark. He headed west
with a stomach full of cabbage.
He hung on the waves. The steep, solvent sea
shot through him, my happy man.
I tuck my head now against the wind
to keep its ashen hand from stroking my chin.
I am in our dark halls & heirlooms.
I pray under Kenmare lace. I lay the two places.
The clock speaks. Tell your daughter,
I am her antecedent. Whether she does the cable
or Trinity stitch, the man whose cheek she kisses
may be gathered into the ocean's net. Tell her,
the clock lashes me at every hour
to the sinking. I am forever infertile by way
of the water, or I would tell my own
all things are endless; there was no first or last
person ever drowned in the ocean.

SELF-PORTRAIT AT GLENDALOUGH

The blackberries are wet on the inside.

The wet Germans are smiling with wet lips in front
of St. Kevin's wet Kitchen.

The Miss Selfridge slicker is the bellman of my collar-
bones, letting in the flashflood.

My blackberry jacket bleeds purple. I go soaking
up headstones. They lean into no wind.

Busy roots blow underground. *Katherine* reclines
to see the underside of a beech

tree. I am what-are-her-bones-like-ing. Petite Kate,
probably. Kathy the Warbler perched on fingers.

Katie of the Lichens with her head in the sand.

That's me at Glendalough.
Me, again, in front of the Round Tower.

There is rain & there is rain. This is both at once.

In the monastic city, the cistern is a black bra.
My wet church has extra seating.

That's a drop of water, blurring me standing firmly
inside myself—an anchoress in the inclement tradition,

a Little Sister of Our Lady Pentax of the Graduation
Gift. I am fluid & filmy. I take the vow

to want to never leave. I take gravel rivulets
toward every roofless thing.

NOTE

"Murray River," uses language from Robert Draper's article "Murray-Darling Basin," which appeared in *National Geographic Magazine*, April 2009.